Arou
Horbury
Richard Bell

WILLOW
ISLAND
EDITIONS

ALSO BY RICHARD BELL

Around Old Ossett

Waterton's Park

Village Walks in West Yorkshire
(Countryside Books)

Yorkshire Rock
(British Geological Survey)

© Richard Bell 1998
Published by Willow Island Editions,
41 Water Lane, Middlestown,
Wakefield, WF4 4PX

www.users.daelnet.co.uk/willowisland

First edition; March 1998
Second edition; August 1998

ISBN 1 902467 00 0

CONTENTS

1. Carr Lodge

The strip cultivation still visible in the ridges and furrows of the Park was probably already in place in 1086 when the Domesday Book surveyors recorded about 40 people and 4 ox-drawn ploughs in 'Orberie' and Crigglestone combined.

The Park was enclosed from the village's North Field when Sunroyd House was built in 1770-1775 for Joseph Bayldon. In 1790 John Carr, lawyer, nephew of the architect, took possession of the property, hence the present name.

Brick tunnels and chambers found by workmen under the Park in 1964 were probably used to store water for the house.

2. St Peter's Convent

The Convent, also known as the House of Mercy, was built between 1862 and 1864, mainly by Henry Woodyer. Starting from a cottage on Millfield Road in 1858, the founder, Harriet Louisa Farrar, established the House as a means of 'rescuing from sin and destruction, the increasing multitude of fallen women who throng the towns . . of this county.'*

The Penny ginnels alongside got their name because the House was known as the 'Penitentiary' by locals.

In the 1920s a Royal patron of the Convent, Princess Marie Louise, was requested not to go walking about the village chatting to the locals as her visits were causing too much of a stir! The nuns embroidered vestments and altar cloths and, until 1988, made communion wafers here.

*Canon John Sharp, cousin of Harriet Louise Farrar, in the first annual report of the House.

ST PET
FROM THE

3. Town Hall

The foundation stone was laid on 30th July 1902 by Joshua Harrop who was presented with a silver trowel and gavel by the architects and builders, Henry Fallas & Sons. A wooden war memorial panel, rescued from old St Peter's School, was recently restored and installed in the Town Hall.

4. Carnegie Free Library

Building commenced in 1905, thanks to a £2,000 grant from the Carnegie Foundation. In the good old days malicious damage to a library book could result in 6 months imprisonment 'with or without hard labour' and, if you were a male under 16, 'with or without whipping'!

Richard Bell 1992

5. Smith's Greengrocer's

Horbury's last gas lamp stood
above a men's urinal which, until
recently, stood behind this lock-up
greengrocers'.

6. Horbury Lawnmowers

Horbury Lawnmowers took over
the Lee & Briggs premises in 1994.

LEE & BRIGGS

Bill head 1951

GENERAL IRONMONGERS
BUILDERS & PLUMBERS MERCHANTS
HEAD OFFICE
WESTFIELD ROAD, HORBURY

It opened in the year before the First World War and was the kind of place where you could still buy gas mantles and wooden planes.

7. Fat Cats wine bar

The United Counties Bank, built in 1910, was later occupied by Barclays Bank. It replaced a cylindrical gentlemens' toilet that stood on the corner and an old shop that sold tripe and peas.

The Temperance Hall (1907 – 1940) still stands on Highfield Road to the left, but now forms part of Nettleton's showrooms. The Nettleton brothers set up their upholstery business in a wooden hut behind the bank in 1919. Also behind the bank, Wilfred Fawcett, boot and shoe maker posted this advertising slogan on a hide of leather; 'LOOK, READ THIS, IF YOU WANT YOUR FEET TO BE SMART THIS SUMMER BRING US YOUR REPAIRS.

Former
United Counties
Bank, Highfield
Road, Horbury. 1910.

13

8. The Town School

(c.1700)

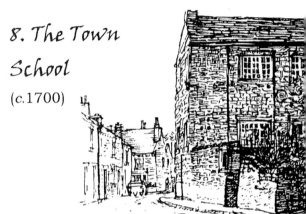

The Penny Readings, performed at the school by, amongst others, Canon John Sharp and his curate Sabine Baring-Gould, were so lively that in 1866 the teachers resolved to engage a policeman 'to take any persons out of the school that misbehaves themselves'.

In 1870, 113 boys and girls paid 3d to 6d a week for their lessons.

9. The Old Lock-up

Miscreants were locked behind the
studded wooden door in a room
furnished with a small stone basin.
The Lock-up was also known as
the Kidcote – a shelter for goats.

10. Tithe Barn

From the car park you can see
some of the timbers of Horbury's
old Tithe Barn which was partly
destroyed by fire in 1904. When

From left to right;
the Old Lock-up
St Leonards
Hospital (behind
Lock-up, not
visible), 1888,
18th century
houses at the end
of Tithe Barn
Street
St Peter's Church,
1794,
buildings on site
of Tithe Barn,
timbers of Tithe
Barn,
Cemetery (closed
1862), now the
car park.

built it stood at the edge of the
village's great West Field, which
stretched from here to Storrs Hill.
A tenth share of produce was
gathered here to support the work
of the parish church.

11. Ring O' Bells Yard

The former Walker's butcher's
shop *(extreme left)* at the entrance
to the Yard was once the 'Ring
O'Bells' public house. A wool

Richard Bell 1992

warehouse dating from 1650
stands behind it in the Yard. The
house with the steps has walls
three feet thick. It's massive,
roughly hewn timbers each stand
on a stack of stone flags.

19

12. St Peter's Church

The Georgian church, which
replaced a Norman chapel, was
built 1790-94 by Horbury born
architect and sometime Lord Mayor
of York, John Carr (1723–1807).
He designed, amongst other
buildings, Heath Hall, Harewood
and Thornes House (destroyed by
fire in the 1950s). The church cost
around £8,000, the bells and organ
a further £2,000.

A former quarryman, Carr made
decorative use of the cross-bedding
patterns in the local sandstone,
notably to give a draped effect on
the Ionic columns of the portico.

Horbury's parish registers record
the burial here of two 'shouldiers',
after the 1643 battle of Wakefield.

Richard Bell
1953

21

13. Old St Peter's School

The old St Peter's Church of England School stood until 1996 to the east of Queen Street. It was founded in 1849 by Canon John Sharp (1810-1903), Horbury's vicar for 65 years, from 1834 to 1899. He was also a mover in the building of the Convent, St Leonard's Hospital, St John's and St Mary's.

During the 1912 miners' strike the school was used as a centre for feeding children. In 1940 pupils had a chance to 'dig for victory' when headmaster Mr J C Douglas was offered a small plot at Green Park for cultivation.

The School moved to Shepstye

Road in 1981. During demolition
of the prefabricated classrooms in
which the school swimming pool
was installed air-raid shelters were
uncovered.

Richard Bell 1993

14. Queen Street

Probably named in honour of
Queen Victoria, Queen Street was
once known as Hodge Lane or
Widgery Lane. The bottom end of
Queen Street beneath the village's
first gas lamp was where the

Queen Street, Horbury

Victoria Prize Band played Christ-
mas carols and Whitsun walkers
gathered. Pill sellers and amateur
dentists had their pitch on the
steps around the lamp. The
Street's 'Tuppeny Shop' has a
carved inscription 'TW 1717'.

15. Fearnside's Yard

Old photographs show a ruined ivy-clad hall standing next to the 1875 'Ebenezer' Primitive Methodist Chapel (now the site of a supermarket) on the High Street on the site of Fearnside's Yard. The Yard, recently re-named Fearnside's Close, was the home of 'Joby' in the 1974 Yorkshire Television film of Stan Barstow's novel.

The 1837 Methodist Free Chapel shown in this drawing was demolished in 1996. It became the Co-operative furniture store some time after the congregation moved to the new United Methodist Chapel (1899) on Highfield Road. This Chapel too has now become a furniture store; Nettleton's Ercol Showrooms.

16. Addingford Steps

The steps go down into a railway
cutting in the Horbury Rock, a type
of sandstone. Addingford tunnel
was removed 1926-1927 to make
the cutting. George Stephenson
(1781-1848) was the engineer of
this stretch of the Manchester and
Leeds Railway (1840).

Richard Bell 1992

29

17. St Mary's Church

This 1893 church by Bodley and Garner has an interior and glass by Kempe. It replaced a mission room set up in 1887 in Forge Lane at the instigation of Miss Goodenough, Mother Superior of the House of Mercy. She was described (by a schoolboy she had once caught in the convent grounds) as a 'grim old warrior' but 'good hearted'.

The church is built of Brighouse sandstone with cornerstones cut from Jurassic oolitic limestone from Weldon, Northamptonshire. Look for the fossil oysters which lived in warm shallow seas 150 million years ago, when sauropod dinosaurs roamed on land.

St Mary's,
Horbury Junction

31

18. St John's Church

Like St Mary's, this church of 1884 had its origins in a mission. At first, in 1864, the congregation met in a room in what is now the Post Office, 'two doors from the "Horse and Jockey"' as the curate, Sabine Baring-Gould (1834-1924), put it. He soon bought land on which the parish hall was built.

Baring Gould wrote the hymn 'Onward, Christian Soldiers' for the 1865 Whitsun procession up Quarry Hill to St Peter's. Exeter born Baring-Gould became well known as an author of novels and folklore studies. He married local mill girl Grace Taylor in 1868.

Stone from Horbury quarry was supplied free for the building of the parish hall by the quarry owner,

Fred Knowles. It was used in the
church too, along with sandstone
from Brighouse and the quarries at
Robin Hood near Rothwell.

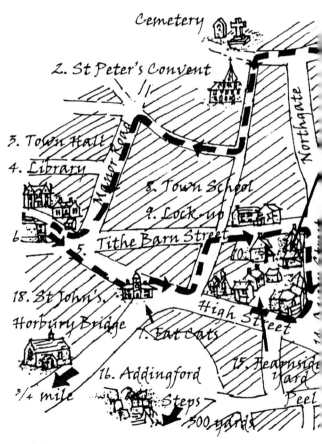

Cemetery

2. St Peter's Convent

3. Town Hall

4. Library

6

5.

18. St John's,

Horbury Bridge

¾ mile

Manor Road

Northgate

8. Town School

9. Lock-up

Tithe Barn Street

10.

High Street

7. Fat Cats

16. Addingford Steps

500 yards

15. Fearnside Yard

Peel

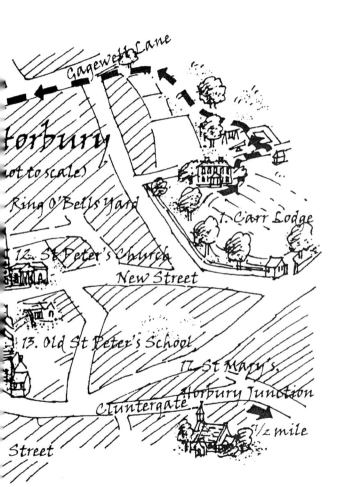

Gagewell Lane

← Gagewell Lane

forbury

(not to scale)

Ring O'Bells Yard

12. St Peter's Church

New Street

1. Carr Lodge

13. Old St Peter's School

11. St Mary's, forbury Junction

Cluntergate

½ mile

Street

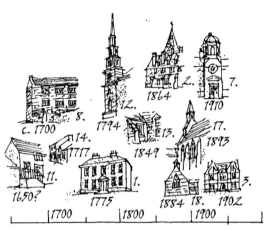

| 1700 | 1800 | 1900 |

Acknowledgements to Local History enthusiast Steve Chapman who runs the class at Horbury School and to Christine M Cudworth, author of *Horbury in Old Photographs*, who kindly proof read my manuscript. I've made much use of *Some Horbury Yesterdays* and *Horbury Heritage* by R D Woodall and also consulted Kate Taylor's *Wakefield District Heritage* and R L Arundale's *A History of Horbury*.

The Drawings are all pen and ink sketches drawn on location by the author between 1983 and 1992, except page 9 which is from a lino-cut made in 1968.